ON DEALING WITH
THE COMMUNIST WORLD

THE ELIHU ROOT LECTURES

ON DEALING
WITH THE
COMMUNIST WORLD

by
GEORGE F. KENNAN

Published for the

COUNCIL ON FOREIGN RELATIONS

by

HARPER & ROW, Publishers

New York and Evanston

COUNCIL ON FOREIGN RELATIONS

The Council on Foreign Relations is a non-profit institution devoted to study of the international aspects of American political, economic and strategic problems. It takes no stand, expressed or implied, on American policy.

The authors of books published under the auspices of the Council are responsible for their statements of fact and expressions of opinion. The Council is responsible only for determining that they should be presented to the public.

For a list of Council publications see pages 56 and 57.

IN MEMORY OF EDWARD JOHN NOBLE

The publication of this volume of the Elihu Root Lectures was aided by a grant from the Edward John Noble Foundation in memory of Mr. Noble and his interest in encouraging American leadership.

FOREWORD

THE LECTURES embodied in this book were written and delivered shortly after my return to this country from some two and a half years of service on behalf of the United States Government in one of the countries of Eastern Europe. This service involved a number of personal encounters, and a good deal of correspondence, with people in the opinion-forming echelons of our public life, devoted to the effort to find understanding for an approach to the problems of the Communist orbit which would look carefully at each of the countries of that area as it exists today, and which would try to identify the hopeful forces and currents of opinion there and then shape policy with a view to encouraging these forces and helping them to become effective in the interests of a more relaxed and safer international life. In the course of these exchanges, I frequently had the impression that the difficulties I encountered lay in deep failures of understanding about certain fundamental elements in the problem of Communist power generally, and that these failures of understanding represented less an inability to absorb and learn the lessons of this decade than to remember those of earlier ones. What troubled me most deeply was the impression gained that large sections of our public were ignorant of the fact that the problems of principle involved in our relations with Communist countries were, in so far as they were generic at all, largely not new; that they had confronted successive administrations from Woodrow Wilson down to F.D.R.; and that there were certain basic lessons learned by experimentation and public debate in earlier days which were relevant to the trials of this one and which, if recognized, could simplify and clarify current policy discussions. It was with a view primarily to refreshing certain of these lessons that the lectures were conceived.

In this sense, the lectures were intended as a contribution to that never-ending discussion which still deals with "Communism" as though it were a single, uniform phenomenon, deserving a single analysis and a single answer. This concept still predominates in our public debates, and so deeply ingrained is it in our Congressional approaches that the slightest attempt to deviate from it raises instantaneous cries of anguish and indignation on the Hill. But I think I should say, to avoid misunderstanding, that in my opinion it is becoming less and less useful.

The term "Communist" still serves a purpose, of course, as a means of distinguishing those countries in which there exist régimes professing to base their programs and policies on the principles of Marxism-Leninism. And what I have tried to suggest in these lectures is that even to the extent this usefulness exists, and to the extent the reader or listener continues to feel that what goes by the name of "Communist" represents something so clearly set apart from the rest of international life as to warrant special and uniform treatment—even to this extent, the problem is neither so new nor so hopeless as is commonly supposed, and there is no substantiation in past experience for the impatient, alarmist and drastic approaches to it that are now being widely entertained in American opinion.

But actually, as I have also tried to suggest in the last of the lectures, things are not really quite this way. As things stand today, the term "Communist" does not serve adequately either to bring out the differences that prevail as between the various "Communist" countries or to make clear the growing degree in which the problems they present for American diplomacy are similar to, or identical with, those presented for us by other countries which do not go by the name of "Communist." To the extent the term may still be useful, the usefulness is a rapidly declining one; and when we insist on deciding things simply according to whether we conceive ourselves to be dealing with something "Communistic" or something "non-Communistic" it is often only ourselves we are deceiving and our own responses we are distorting.

If I myself have used the term "Communist" here, it is because I remember too well the number of occasions on which, when I tried to argue the need for discriminating policies toward Jugoslavia, people have disposed of my argument to their own satisfaction by saying: "Well, they're Communists, aren't they?"—and because, in the light of such attitudes, I know no other language in which these matters can be usefully discussed. But I would like, in consigning the lectures to the reading public, to apologize for this rather shabby compromise with contemporary semantics, and to say that I think there could be no more useful innovation in the discussion, public and governmental, of the affairs of the "Communist" orbit than a law which forbad all of us, including myself, to use the word "Communist" at all, and forced us to treat the régimes and peoples of each of these countries specifically, for what they are—which is something much more highly differentiated, as among themselves, and something much less differentiated from what exists elsewhere, than we commonly suppose.

GEORGE F. KENNAN

Princeton, N.J.
December 1963

CONTENTS

ON DEALING WITH
THE COMMUNIST WORLD

1
THE RATIONALE
OF COEXISTENCE

W HEN I first conceived the thought of addressing myself, in these lectures, to the subject matter you see suggested by their titles, I was acting under a sense of irritation over what seemed to me to be the lack of historical depth in much of what was being said publicly in this country about the respective problems concerned. I had only recently returned from a long absence abroad. Much of what was being said here was new to me. When I was told, for example, that a prominent American political figure was advocating the withdrawal of diplomatic representation from—in effect the breaking of relations with—the Soviet Government and other Communist governments, my first reaction was: God help us! Is not this where we came in thirty years ago— thirty years ago this month, in fact—when F.D.R. took the step of recognizing the Soviet Government and when it fell to me, very young and very excited, to accompany our first ambassador to the Soviet Union, Mr. William C. Bullitt, on his first official journey to Moscow? And was this action of F.D.R.'s not actually the culmination of a fifteen-year debate over the whole question of recognition? And did we not all assume that the debate had at least found its final and timely termination with this act of recognition, whether we liked it or not? Or, to take another example, when I noted that one of our leading conservative columnists was referring to us as being "at war" with the Soviet Union, my heart fell; because I thought of the years of effort, the reams of paper, the entire libraries, in fact, of published materials, which had been devoted to the search for a more meaningful and constructive definition than this of the nature of our relationship to Soviet power, one that did better justice to the complexity of the problem. And I thought: does this, too, all have to be gone over again? Do we have to start once more with all the arguments and counter-arguments of 1918, as though our minds constituted some sort of a *tabula rasa*—as though we had just woken up from some sort of amnesia and were amazed to find an ideologically hostile force glaring at us over the fence?

This, as I say, is the way I began. But I must confess that as I went along I became aware that things more serious than mere shallowness of historical memory were involved in some of these utterances I had stumbled upon. It became evident to me that we had to do here with a great and important body of opinion in this country—and a growing one, I fear—which was fully prepared to reject in its entirety the experience and judgment of all of us who have had to deal responsibly with the problem of Communist power over these past thirty years—a body of opinion which was prepared to throw both hope and patience to the wind, to embrace an outlook which rejected every possibility other than the most relentless and embittered and uncompromising struggle, and to pursue a policy which, in my profound conviction, could lead only, and with inexorable logic, to the final and irreparable disaster which is in all our minds. I became aware, in short, that we had to do here, in the question of our relation to world Communism, with a crisis of opinion of such seriousness as to constitute of itself a great and present danger.

If then, in talking of these things in this first lecture, I speak less from a platform of academic detachment than from that of an engaged and troubled citizen, this is my reason for doing so.

WHAT I should like to talk about today is the familiar subject of coexistence, which lies at the heart of this whole matter. There is a great and real issue here. It is the question whether it should be the goal of our national policy to achieve the early and total destruction, everywhere, of everything that calls itself Communism, even if this goal has to be pursued at the expense of our chances for living with Communist power successfully so long as it is not destroyed. Or whether it should be our goal to find acceptable ways of living with it, and influencing it, even if this has to be done at the expense of our chances for destroying it entirely.

For many years I was under the impression that the first of these views—the one that despairs of living successfully with our adversary and seeks only his destruction—had been debated and tried in earlier times and that there had crystallized among us an adequate consensus to the effect that this was not the most hopeful way to approach our problem. From 1933 to the late 1940s this was, I think, the case. But during the past ten years we have witnessed the resurgence of a body of opinion which takes the other line, which rejects in effect the whole concept of peaceful coexistence and which would commit us to a policy of "we or they"—a policy which sees no issue to the present contest except in the final and complete destruction of one side or the other.

Both of the views I cited earlier as evidences of historical shallowness fall, as you will note, into this category as well. And they are not isolated examples. Such outlooks are held by a great many people around the country. They have a strong and growing hold on much of our student youth. There are entire geographic regions where they have almost a clean sweep, and where to challenge them at all is to court resentment, misunderstanding, and obloquy. They have rarely affected the attitudes of those who, confronted with over-all responsibility for the conduct of foreign policy, have had to look at these matters long and hard.

and to take the rap for their decisions. But they have made deep inroads on those aspects of our national behavior which are directly subject to Congressional action or influence—such things as security procedures, visa and passport controls, trade restrictions, export and shipping controls. In this way they have often served to cancel out or to weaken the policy the executive branch was trying, at the moment, to follow. So strong is now their prevalence in Congress and certain other segments of government in Washington that it is not an exaggeration to say that we have today two wholly different and mutually contradictory foreign policies being pursued simultaneously in that city, and you can find whichever of them you want, depending on which door you want to put your head in.

No one will be under any doubt, I am sure, as to my own position with relation to these two alternatives. This is not the first time I have had occasion to raise my voice publicly against these counsels of despair which persist in viewing Communism as the only serious evil in the world, which refuse to recognize in it the elements of either change or differentiation, which insist on treating it as a single conspiratorial force, dedicated only to our destruction and beyond the range of any human appeals, and which, accordingly, would willingly see us sacrifice all the positive values of life to the struggle against it. Naturally, I have to regret that such views still exist and still have the wide currency they do.

But what worries me even more is the combination of amused contempt, or cynicism, or dreamlike complacency, with which I find this outlook treated by most of my friends. I do not think this body of thought can be disposed of by silence or by ridicule.

The question it raises is not a disrespectable one. There *is* this thing called Communist power. There *is* this problem of its hostility toward us. It is a great problem. And if to myself and to many of those who hear or read these lectures, the basic considerations affecting our answer are reasonably obvious, there are plainly a great many people to whom they are not. If these people ever knew the reasons why something called "victory," in the sense of an early and complete elimination of "Communism," is not the answer, they have forgotten them. And I sometimes suspect that many of us who think that we understand these reasons very well might be hard put to it to recall exactly what they were.

Let us therefore take up this question once more. Let us accept the fact that we have this sharp and serious challenge, and let us ask ourselves, as though we had never asked it before: Why, indeed, coexistence? Why not victory?

No objective historian would deny, I think, that the attitude with which the Soviet leaders initially approached the societies and governments of the West was an outrageous one, full of prejudice and intellectual arrogance and intolerable hostility. It was not the same kind of challenge, to be sure, as those common to international life up to that point. It corresponded to none of the established concepts of international hostility. It was aimed, in theory, only against certain classes in the West, not against entire peoples. It did not envisage overt and full-fledged international hostilities. But it did involve attitudes which were insulting and menacing to the Western societies, which had as their aim the violent destruction of the political systems of those societies, and which were clearly unacceptable on any normal standards of international life.

There could be no question in 1918, and there can be none today, of the moral right of a society to defend itself against such designs: to take measures for the disarming and control of subversive elements within its own citizenry, and to take measures of military precaution insofar as these might be responsive to the nature of the challenge.

But it became clear at an early date that if you went beyond this defensive effort, as some of our allies halfheartedly tried to do in the various interventions of 1918 to 1920, and as many people in this country wanted us to do, and made it your objective to overthrow the Soviet Government, you got yourself into a very messy business indeed, even from the standpoint of moral and political responsibility. There were unclarities and ambiguities in the relationship of the Soviet régime to the Russian people which constantly confused the issue. You discovered that the attitudes of people to régime—and particularly the question whether people really wanted to be liberated from it—depended largely on what they thought were, at any given point, the possible alternatives. But these alternatives were often highly obscure. The two greatest non-Communist political parties which had existed in Russia prior to the Communist seizure of power there, hated each other, unfortunately, at least as much as they hated the Communists. It was out of the question that they could ever get together; and neither, as it happened, was capable of governing alone. Those who spoke, therefore, of overthrowing the Soviet Government had no very convincing answers as to what would be put in its place. The problem was not disposed of merely by saying that democratic procedures would be permitted to prevail. This principle had been tried in 1917; but the understanding for democratic procedures among the Russian people had turned out to be not very widespread. A single ruthless minority had easily pushed through the entire parliamentary system. It was not even certain that some of the opponents of Bolshevism had a much greater devotion than did the Bolsheviki to democratic ideals.

Not only that, but you found that a very considerable part of the Russian people preferred to take their chances on adjusting peaceably to Communist rule rather than to have someone try to liberate them by force and in this way compel them to accept all the hardships and dangers and, above all, the excruciating political choices that go with a civil war and particularly one in which foreigners are involved. It was questionable, in fact, how many people in Russia you were going to be benefiting by such an interference into their political life. That some would be pleased to have this effort made was clear; but that many others would not was also clear. On balance, it was a real question whether such an undertaking, even if successful in the negative sense of bringing about the expulsion of the Communists from the seats of power in Moscow, would have been a blessing for the people as a whole or merely a new source of hardship and horror. One should remember that even the half-hearted and futile little military expeditions which the allies did dispatch to Russian soil in 1918 got vast numbers of people into very serious trouble; the executions that followed them numbered in the tens of thousands.

But aside from all these questions of the political propriety and usefulness of such an endeavor, it was clear that in the sheer physical sense it was an extremely unpromising undertaking. The Russian Communist Party, having had years of experience in the techniques of ousting others from the seats of power, showed from the start an extraordinary mastery of the science of clinging to these seats itself. Once the Communists had established the monopoly of their rule, they had little diffulty in spiking in the bud any really serious attempts at armed opposition. It was plain that they could be removed from the seats of power only by a major insertion of outside force. But any such outside intervention was bound to confuse the very political situation to which it was addressed; for nobody, however opposed to his own government, really feels very comfortable associating himself with foreign military forces coming onto the territory of his country. And the task, in the sheer military sense, was bound to be an enormous one. What was involved, if the intervention was going to do any real good, was not just driving the Communists from power in Moscow. This alone would not have finished them. They were not that breed of cat. They were skilled, as few political movements in history have ever been, in the arts of underground political activity. They knew exactly how to go underground. They would have had to be pursued to the ends of the vast Russian land; and nothing suggests that foreign armies endeavoring to accomplish that pursuit would have ended up in any better position than did, say, the Japanese in the Communist-penetrated areas of northern China during the last war—riveted to the railways, harassed and bled at every turn by guerrillas having closer links with the people and knowing precisely how to exploit those links to the discomfort of an outside force. And this is not to mention the two great subjective questions as to whether, if this were conceived as a joint western undertaking, allied unity would ever have been sufficient to sustain it (it certainly was not in

1918), or if it were to be done by a single Western power, what Western public would ever have consented to bear for long a burden of this nature.

I mention these things simply in order to make the point that even in the early days of Bolshevism, when the Soviet régime was relatively weak and inexperienced, the idea of its overthrow, as a direct goal of Western policy, was never a promising one—either from the standpoint of military feasibility or from that of political effectiveness. Think, then, by comparison, what it would be today, when the Soviet régime has enjoyed a monopoly of power in Russia for nearly half a century; when it has behind it several decades of political and administrative experience; when it disposes over some of the strongest armed forces in the world; and when it has unquestionably achieved a far higher degree of acceptance than was the case in those early years; when large segments of the Soviet population, in fact, have never known any other political system and would be incapable of conceiving of any alternative to this one. The moral is that even if the nature of Russian Communism had undergone no change—even if it represented exactly the same sort of challenge to us that it did forty years ago (which incidentally is what our ardent liberationists all seem to assume), I should have deepest misgivings about any concept of policy which envisaged, as a sort of an end-product, the overthrow of Soviet power either by the direct use of our forces or by incitement of subject peoples to revolts which we would be vaguely expected to back up if they got into trouble.

I am sorry to have to plunge this way into what seem to be murky and somewhat speculative depths, but these unhappy realities seem to lie at the heart of our problem; for it is hard to conceive of any liberationist policy which would not, sooner or later, run up against them at some point. We are told, for example, by prominent protagonists of the liberationist view, that to achieve the downfall of Communism, we would not have to occupy Russia or China. The vast majority of people in these countries, they assure us, are not Communists. "They will, with proper guidance, take care of their own freedom once they are

released from the iron grip of Communist dictatorship." But such
a statement raises more questions than it solves. Who, first of
all, is to release them from their iron grip? They, themselves?
Scarcely. Popular revolt against a ruthless, experienced modern
dictatorship, which enjoys a monopoly over weapons and com-
munications, which has its own armed forces under tight control,
and which retains its unity and its will to power, is simply not a
possibility in the modern age.

And could the peoples of these countries be depended upon
to "take care of their own freedom" even if, by some miracle, that
grip *was* loosened? This only raises again the tedious question of
the possible alternative to Communism. There are no opposition
parties in Russia today. There is no fund of political experience
outside the Communist Party itself. Russia's previous experience
with the concepts of Western democracy was pathetically brief and
shallow; and the people who would remember it are mostly gone.
The organized political force that could replace the Soviet Communist Party in that vast area today is simply not visible. I would
know of no assurance that whatever might conceivably come in
place of what is there now would be any closer to liberal ideals.
Are we, then, to take moral responsibility for this incalculable
change, which may or may not be for the better from the standpoint of the average Russian?

I personally believe that political change will continue to come
to Russia; and important change at that. But if it is a question of
our own time, I can conceive of its coming, as to some extent it
already has, only on the foundation of and within the framework
of the present political system, which is now firmly established
and which has shaped the political outlooks and assumptions of
an entire generation.

But while we are on this subject of political change in Russia,
there is one further wrinkle of which I think we should take
cognizance. We have here in this country, among the opponents
of coexistence, people who argue with great vehemence that
there *is* indeed a political alternative to the Soviet régime; that
it exists in the form of the non-Russian minorities within the

traditional Russian state. These elements, they claim, are thirsting for independence. We could bring about the overthrow of Soviet Communism by supporting them politically—by encouraging them to fight for their independence with the implicit promise of our support—by encouraging them, in other words, not only to destroy Communist rule in Russia but indeed to achieve the permanent break-up of the traditional Russian state.

There can be no denying that the multi-national composition which has characterized both the former Russian Empire and the Soviet Union—particularly the Soviet Union since 1945—is an important political fact. Unquestionably, the unhappiness of non-Russian elements had much to do with the final break-up of Tsardom. It is not at all silly to suggest that this factor may well have an important bearing on the political future of the traditional Russian area. But this is about all one can say with any degree of certainty.

Yet the thesis with which we are now confronted on the part of many of these American "liberationists" goes far beyond this. It asserts with a great show of definiteness that there are known to be a whole series of national groups within the Soviet Union which have long desired independence and which dispose over the necessary prerequisites for an independent existence but which were deprived of that independence by the Soviet régime. They even name a number of entities which allegedly correspond to this description; the list will be found in the so-called Captive Nations Resolution, to which a majority of the members of our Congress—many of them having only the dimmest ideas of the places or peoples involved—were induced to subscribe in 1959.

It is not to deny sympathy for the national feelings of certain of the peoples concerned if I point out that as a question of fact this claim is grossly exaggerated, and in some respects entirely spurious.

There are indeed instances—and I am thinking here particularly of the Baltic states—where a good case could be made for the validity of such claims. But there are other instances in which the whole thesis is fictitious and ludicrous. Certain of the national groups whose names appear in the Captive Nations Resolution as those of nations thirsting for a lost independence never existed at all in this quality; and it is incomprehensible that the Congress of the United States should have been led to commit the policy of this country formally to something called their liberation. Finally, there are still other instances in which we simply do not know the facts. We are often told, for example, that the Ukrainians are all thirsting for complete separation from the traditional Russian state. Perhaps so. But who knows? There has been, and could have been, no proper formal test of opinion on this point over these past forty-five years. The Ukraine never was really independent. History bears no evidence that the majority of the people of the Ukraine have at any time desired a total separation from the main body of the Russian people. And those who assure us that this is the case are for the most part people who have had no personal contact with the central regions of the Ukraine for many years, if ever.

Even should these claims be far better substantiated as assertions of objective fact than they actually are, I can think of nothing more catastrophic than that the policy of our government should be committed to the break-up of the traditional Russian state. Remember that nothing of this sort could be carried forward except at the cost of the violent and total estrangement of the Russian people, at the cost of their embittered armed opposition, at the cost, in fact, of a Russian civil war which would make that of 1918–1920 look like child's play. Nor would the chances of the non-Russian elements be favorable in any such encounter unless they had the foreign assistance on a massive scale. The Great Russians may or may not constitute a majority on the present territory of the Soviet Union, but they constitute by far the strongest national group; they command the traditional seats of political power; they command the centers of transportation and communication. In many of the areas where other nationalities predominate, Russians are heavily intermingled with the non-Russian population. Not only would outside force have to be invoked on a massive scale in order to bring about any such dismemberment of Russia in the first instance, but this outside force would have to remain indefinitely in occupation in order to enforce the maintenance of a *status quo* so violently unacceptable to the strongest national group in the area.

If the dream of popular revolt in the Soviet Union is today unreal in any case, which it is, it becomes doubly unreal if you think of it as hinged to an American commitment to the dismemberment of traditional Russia; for in this case all hope of the achievement of a peaceful consensus among the inhabitants of the region would have been lost; the strongest national element would have been wholly antagonized; and once again, the hatreds engendered over issues not connected with Communism would overshadow any resentment felt towards the Soviet régime.

We have, finally, among the arguments against coexistence, the insistent assertion that the Soviet leaders are largely bluffing and could easily be brought to desist from their undertakings or to yield ill-gotten gains if only we had the gumption to tell them that the alternative is war. This is a thesis which has received a specious appearance of substantiation from the fact that the Soviet government, confronted last year with a choice between withdrawing certain of its installations in Cuba or becoming involved in a war with the United States, preferred to withdraw the installations, and did so at some cost to its prestige.

I can only warn in the strongest way against attempting to draw inferences of this sort from the Cuban crisis. Whatever else may be said of the Russian Communists, history affords no substantiation for the suggestion that they are cowards. If every gesture of prudence or moderation on their part is to be hailed as proof of their faint-heartedness, and cited as an argument for bolder military pressures from our side, I shudder to contemplate the implications for the future course of Soviet–American relations.

The Soviet government is a great power, with a far-flung and complex pattern of international interests, involvements, and commitments. Like any other great power, it can be put on the spot. It can be placed in situations where to yield to bald military threats or ultimata would involve consequences disastrous and unacceptable. Nothing in the long history of its behavior suggests that it would yield, or could afford to yield, to this sort of open intimidation. In general, that school of American political thinking which views the East–West conflict in terms of apocalyptic visions of someone achieving a momentary superiority in weaponry and then saying to others, "Now you do what we say or else . . ." reflects a very shallow understanding indeed of what makes this world go around. We would not react to this sort of thing, and neither would the others.

The fact is that all these ideas for some sort of violent and short-term disposal of the Soviet problem—disposal of it in ways that would spare us the necessity of talking and dealing and compromising with people whose views we don't like—all these ideas lead sooner or later to war. Let there be no mistake about this. It is going to be hard enough, in the best of circumstances, to preserve the peace. Let no one suppose it will be easier to do so if the very idea of accommodation is ruled out. There is always some point between the undertaking and completion of these militant schemes at which the outbreak of hostilities would become inevitable. And it must be emphasized that the moment we get to this point there become valid and operable, once more, all those ambiguities and uncertainties which were discussed earlier in connection with the very idea of overthrowing the Soviet government by force. Because war has to have an object. There have to be war aims. If you conduct military operations, you have to be willing to state what you would settle for. And what would our war aims be? Is there any likelihood that, once involved in hostilities, we would be inclined to settle for limited aims—for anything less than the complete destruction of Soviet power? The experience of two world wars would not suggest it. In each of these cases we heeded the demands of the hotheads and the super-patriots, and we insisted in fighting the conflict to its final and ultimate conclusion of the total destruction of the enemy's military strength and his political system: in one case, at the cost of installing the Communists in power in Russia; and in the other case, at the cost of turning over to them half of Europe.

And during both of these contests, people in our midst who suggested a compromise peace, as did Lord Lansdowne in 1917, were treated as little short of treasonable.

🎵🎵🎵

Now THERE are two things I have refrained from mentioning up to this point, not because they were not germane to the discussion, but because I wanted, if I could, to make my points without them. The first is the element of change in the Soviet Union. It affects what I have said because it is this that tells us that these desperate and militant policies are not only unpromising but also unnecessary.

This is a great subject in itself. I shall only say here that I find it amazing that men can seriously discuss today these questions of our attitude toward Communist power without taking account of this factor. One can argue about the exact nature and extent of this change; but I do not see how anyone can dispute the difference between the weak and isolated Soviet state of the 1920s and the 1930s and the great power we have before us today, with its far-flung interests and involvements, its embarrassments of empire, its obligations of alliance, its new personalities, and its evolving internal problems. This, surely, is something far more like the traditional, established great power of "Russia" than like the fanatical political personality we faced in the Soviet régime of Lenin's time or the nightmarish totalitarian despotism of Stalin.

We have no need to be thrown off balance by such things as Khrushchev's statement that he would bury us. This does not really mean that he expects to finish us off within his time. He is to much of a realist for this. This, as I see it, was simply a prediction: that his political system would live to assist at the funeral of ours, not vice versa. This is a prediction basic to the Marxist outlook. He cannot do other than to reiterate it. He cannot explain publicly that this is all he means by it; he is a political person and his dogmatist critics would take advantage of it. But there is no reason we should not recognize it for what it is.

I find a great deal that is troublesome in the ideas and behavior of the present Soviet state. There is still a great deal in the way of established procedure and inherited prejudice that Moscow will have to get over before the Soviet Union can coexist tranquilly with other nations. But if I had to choose between dealing with this one or the one we faced thirty years ago, I would take this one any day. While its evolution may not proceed at the pace we would like, it has proceeded at a pace which affords no grounds at all for the total abandonment of all hope that it may some day take an acceptable place in the family of nations. And nothing in the state at which it has arrived justifies us in viewing it as something so far outside the range of ordinary experience that we are entitled to cast aside all the decencies when we deal with it.

The second point I have delayed mentioning, or invoking as an argument, is that enormous multiplication of the dangers of war, and of the unsuitability of war as a weapon of policy, which we have before us in the phenomenon of the nuclear weapon of long-range destructive capacity. I have deliberately refrained from introducing this subject; for what I wish to emphasize is that the concept of destroying Soviet power entirely, as a major goal of policy, is and has always been inherently unsound, quite aside from the nuclear factor. It was unsound in 1918 when the allied expeditionary forces went to Russia. It was unsound in 1941 when Hitler's vast conventional armed forces launched themselves upon the Soviet Union. It did not take the atomic weapon to produce this situation. We only confuse ourselves when we ascribe that quality to the weapon.

The presence on this earth today of systems of weaponry suicidal in their implications strikes me as being only a sharp and impatient reminder by the Almighty of a reality which ought to have been visible to us all long ago, which ought, in fact, to have been visible on the example of World War I, but which we stubbornly refused to see: and this is the very narrow and limited degree to which force can ever be the main solution for problems that involve the states of mind—the outlooks and convictions—of great masses of people on this planet. I am startled and disturbed when I hear it said, as I sometimes do, by our military strategists and commentators, that our purpose in war is simply to "kill Germans" or to "kill Russians" or to "kill" whomever else it may be considered to be our enemy. Is this really the purpose of warfare? Are we really served—do American purposes really prosper—just because a life is extinguished, somewhere on this earth, in the agony of battle? And do they prosper in proportion to the number of lives thus extinguished? I cannot believe it. The sources of tragedy in international life lie in the differences of outlook that divide the human race; and it seems to me that our purposes prosper only when something happens in the mind of another person, and perhaps in our own mind as well, which makes it easier for all of us to see each other's problems and prejudices with detachment and to live peaceably side by side. The question is not: Why not victory? The question is: What does the word "victory" mean?

I am not preaching a spineless pacifism. Such is the stubbornness and recalcitrance of human nature that the use of force cannot always be foreign to the process of persuasion. Force, too, has its place as an argument, but only a limited place. Force can never be the main argument, or the only one. With it must come, if it is to have any eloquence at all, such things as understanding and patience and the willingness to persuade and, above all, the readiness to restrict force to minimum dimensions and to stop it at the right time.

The trouble with all these proposals for the angry, the militant, the punitive approach is that they ignore the dialectics necessarily involved in every great effort to exert influence on the international scene. They neglect the fact that the hopeful approaches have always to be dialectical ones, embracing contradictory elements, embracing both repulsion and attraction, pressure and conciliation, the readiness to defend where defense is the only answer, but also the readiness to receive, to listen, to concede, to be generous, to take chances, and to give confidence, even while defending.

These suggestions that we should solve our problem by getting angry, by getting tough, by doing something drastic and abrupt, are invidious not just because they involve procedures and concepts which are unpracticable and unfeasible and from which the authors would themselves be obliged to desist, if they ever found themselves in positions of responsibility—they are invidious in an even worse way because they crowd and damage and deflate the hopeful approaches, rob them of their effectiveness and their credibility. The Captive Nations Resolution has freed no captive nations, nor is it likely to do so. But it has irritated and misled and estranged a great many people, including numbers who were by no means Communists. It has given a serious misimpression to our friends as well as our adversaries. It has played into the hands of the hotheads and fanatics on both sides. It has complicated the task of everyone in our government who has been working to avoid the catastrophe of war. And the same could be said for many other of the manifestations of the *simpliste*, die-hard psychology which it reflects. My principal charge against this outlook is not that it is itself without hopeful perspectives, though this too is true. My charge is that, uncorrected, unchallenged, and permitted to have the currency it has in this country today, it cripples the hopefulness of any other approach.

This is why I think it high time that the country clarified its mind on the basic issue of coexistence. If we genuinely wish to avoid the catastrophes of a nuclear war and to find solutions to our differences with world Communism which will render redundant and dispensable the tremendous burden of armaments now resting on mankind, it will not do to let a great part of the vocal segment of our society go on talking as though the search for possibilities of accommodation were unnecessary and undesirable, and anyone who facilitates it were unpatriotic. I submit that a constructive and hopeful policy toward the Soviet Union cannot be conducted against the background of so massive a failure of understanding—against the background of such irresolution and such divided counsel as mark this country today. This is not a question of Russia alone. Behind the Soviet Union there stands as well the great problem of relations with Communist China, to which all the considerations adduced in the lecture will some day be relevant, if they are not now.

If what we require is a new national debate, and something like a public showdown, to clarify these questions and permit this country to speak with a clear and unequivocal voice in world affairs, then let us not postpone this debate any longer. This is a question of fundamentals. Whichever way you cut it, someone—and by that I mean one of two great bodies of thought in our country—is terribly, tragically, and intolerably wrong. If we are to move ahead effectively, the country will have to make up its mind which it is.

2

EAST–WEST
TRADE

In the first of these occasions I gave my reasons for believing that the West has no choice but to accept the quest for peaceful coexistence as the basis for policy toward the countries of the Communist world. Today, I would like to talk about one aspect of coexistence, namely, that of commercial exchanges between Communist and non-Communist countries, which is always with us and which poses some of the most difficult and baffling problems for Western statesmanship.

The problem of what is called East–West trade is scarcely a new one. For forty-six years our statesmen, and those of other Western countries, have been facing it in one form or another. So long and deep is the experience with it that one is taken aback, sometimes, to see to what extent it is treated in our own public debates as a new problem, and to what extent the lessons and precedents of the past are ignored.

Admittedly, these lessons are of limited value. Insofar as they derive from the prewar period, they relate, of course, only to the Soviet Union—and only to a Soviet Union in isolation, at that. Today, we have a wide spectrum of Communist countries to face, and in almost every case the problem presents certain specific features. There have, too, been important subjective changes on our side which have to be taken into account. But there are certain elements of this early experience of trade with an isolated Soviet Union which ought perhaps to be borne in mind in any discussion of the wider problem of today; and it will be well to mention them at the start.

First, there is the fact that in the period following the consolidation of Communist power in Russia most Western governments, after looking at the problem long and hard, and under the buffeting of much public debate, settled for policies which drew a distinction between normal trade, where value was received for value, on the one hand, and one-sided favors, such as long-term credits, grants, aid, etc., on the other; and they showed a disposition, in general, to permit normal trade but to withhold the favors. This was the policy of the United States government, as of others, in the period before World War II; and the basic reasons for it are fairly clear. To extend favors to an ideologically hostile country could scarcely be defended, on political grounds; and, except for the insistent Soviet effort to obtain long-term credits, there was little demand or incentive for anything of this nature. "Foreign aid," prior to World War II, was not yet a concept. On the other hand, it was also not feasible, as a rule, to forbid one's own businessmen to take advantage of favorable trading opportunities that came their way, especially where the other side was prepared to give value for value. In addition, there was at no time sufficient solidarity or self-discipline among Western nations to make possible a unified policy in restraint of such trade. If one's own businessmen did not take the trade, somebody else's businessmen did. The result was that normal trade with the U.S.S.R. became a standard feature of the international economic relations of practically every Western country. The statesmen of the 1920s and 1930s would have been amazed to find that the simple principle involved in this practice was being so widely questioned today.

Secondly, trade with Russia never became a very important factor in the economic life of the West. It found its limits in the dimensions of the Soviet capacity of pay. In the absence of any sort of convertibility, this capacity was largely identical with the portion of Soviet production which the Soviet government was able or disposed to make available for export, plus the available gold production of the Soviet Union; and these items were never very great. In the years from 1921 through 1938, Soviet foreign trade averaged only 1.5 per cent of world trade—a small percentage for a country that occupied one-sixth of the world's surface.

The economic significance of what was then called "trade with Russia" was greater in the case of certain other Western countries, notably Germany and England, than in the case of the United States. The turnover of American trade with Soviet Russia ran only in the order of something like $100 million per annum. The Germans, on the other hand, had at times an important volume of machine-tool exports to the Soviet Union, particularly important against the background of the economic crisis of the 1930s; and British imports from Russia, particularly of timber, were of more than minor dimensions. In general, however, the volume of trade with Soviet Russia was not such as to justify the predictions either of the optimists, who saw it assuming dimensions which would constitute a major boon to Western exporters, or of the pessimists, who had visions of the Western markets being swamped and distorted by vast onslaughts of Soviet dumping.

Thirdly, the technical dangers of permitting private firms in a capitalist country to deal with the foreign trade monopoly of an ideologically hostile government proved not to be very great— certainly not great enough to justify the lively fears entertained in Western circles when the Soviet government first appeared as a trading partner on the world scene. It was clear that such dangers did exist, and had to be guarded against. But Western firms turned out to be pretty well capable of looking after themselves; and where this seemed to be required, as in the case of the German machinery manufacturers or the British timber importers, they found ways of mutual collaboration to guard against their being unduly played off against each other by a stronger trading partner.

These, in the main, were the lessons of the earlier experience of trade with the Soviet Union. They are cited here because all are germane, in some degree, to the problems of the present.

〰〰〰

IN THE recent period, the problems posed for Western statesmanship in this area have been extremely complex, because they
are widely differentiated both geographically and functionally.
There are a number of different countries or groupings of countries, each of which presents a specific problem from the standpoint of United States policy; and yet there are also certain
considerations affecting entire categories of commodities, such as
wheat and oil, which have to be taken into account in dealings
with the Soviet bloc as a whole. And in addition to this, the
problem is different, in many instances, for our allies in the West
and East than it is for us; and this raises for us the question of not
just what *our* policy should be at any given point, but of what
attitude we should take toward the policies of our allies and
friends.

Some of these complexities will become evident if one glances
at the various geographic entities involved and notes the special
situations with which they confront us.

Let us begin with the Soviet Union itself. Here, we have a
long tradition of trade; but, as we have just noted, it has always
been trade of modest dimensions. Neither for the West nor for
the Soviet government has it ever had more than a minor
economic significance. Since the recent war it has been even
further inhibited by the heightened sensitivity of United States
opinion to the idea of shipping to the Soviet Union anything that
could conceivably contribute to the growth of Soviet military
strength. This has resulted in an elaborate system of American
and NATO export controls, reinforced by the provisions of the
Battle Act. These measures may have had some effect in slowing
down the rate of advance in Soviet military strength. It is doubt-
ful that they could have done much more. There is little, other
than the most highly classified sorts of weaponry, and particularly
little when it comes to such things as machine tools and other
semi-military goods, which the Soviet government cannot acquire
either from or through neutral countries or by mastering the

necessary techniques and developing the respective production itself, if it sets its mind to it. The significance of these export controls, accordingly, has probably lain more in the subjective satisfaction they have afforded to American opinion than in such objective effect as they may have had. But the states of mind behind them have tended, and still tend, to inhibit any extensive development of United States–Soviet trade; and these states of mind have to be taken into account as an important environmental factor.

Recently, a complication has come into this situation in the form of the sudden readiness of the Soviet government to buy wheat abroad. They, of course, have a great shortage of it—and the United States a great surplus. Both shortage and surplus are the effect of irrational agricultural policies pursued by the two governments for ideological reasons. Neither government is really inclined to depart from these policies merely in order to avoid the shortage or the surplus, as the case might be. In these circumstances, the basis for a deal, or a series of deals, would seem, on the face of it, to be very much present. The United States, by selling its wheat, would make it possible for the Russians to go on giving their farmers inadequate incentive for the production of grain; they, by purchasing it, would make it possible for the United States to go on giving its own farmers too much.

The American statesmen of earlier decades would have been amazed to learn that there could be any hesitation about so obviously advantageous a proposition. In those earlier days, the complaint used to be that the Russians bought only prototypes for industrial equipment, and refused to buy consumer goods; this was cited as evidence that the trade had no proper stability. Now, the Russians have come into the market for consumer goods, and yet numerous echelons of the United States government have had to be occupied for weeks with the decision whether to permit even one such deal to take place. In this, one has an example of the extent to which in the United States the whole question of trade with the Soviet Union has recently become a focal point for political and emotional hesitations.

Turning to the Eastern European satellites, one has a still different set of problems. There is, above all, the general question of whether one wishes to make it easier for these countries to achieve a measure of independence and flexibility in their foreign economic relations, looking not only eastward but also westward for their opportunities; or whether it should be the Western objective to deny them, wherever we can, access to Western markets, both as buyers and sellers, in the hope that this will hamper their economic progress, and embarrass their governments. This last policy, naturally, tends to deprive them of any hope that the West could be of help to them in working out their economic future, and to convey to them that however distasteful the prospect may be (and in some instances it seems very distasteful indeed) they have no choice but to stick closely to the Soviet Union and to look predominantly in that direction for their future economic connections. Both views appear to be represented in Washington; but the second one seems generally to have prevailed when it came to Congressional determinations of one sort or another. This is, of course, a profoundly political question, and one which cuts to the heart of the problem of coexistence, with particular relation to polycentrism. But it is a question to which policy-makers are simply obliged to find answers, because until one answers it, one cannot know whether one should apply to the satellites the same policy concepts one applies to the Soviet Union, or different ones.

A still further problem is presented by Jugoslavia. Here is a country which is not a member of the Soviet bloc and where most of the specific objections raised in the West to the attitudes and conduct of the bloc countries do not apply. Yet there is strong sentiment in the United States Congress for denying to Jugoslavia normal commercial treatment and for doing everything possible, by means of tariff barriers and moral suasion on our own business community, to exclude Jugoslav goods from access to our market. Here, again, the basic question is actually the same one that presents itself in the case of the satellites: whether, namely, one wishes to encourage Communist countries to find independent answers to their economic problems or whether one wishes them to look exclusively to Moscow for these answers. Because the satellites watch the Jugoslav experience very closely, and if one is to penalize normal Jugoslav trade with the West, merely on the grounds that the Jugoslavs continue to call themselves Communists, the satellites can only conclude from this example that even if they were to go a great deal further than any of them have gone or could afford to go in detaching themselves from Moscow's political orbit, this would still not be enough to win them even normal commercial treatment at Western hands.

To all these problems, both with Russia and with the Communists countries of Eastern Europe, a new depth of complexity is added by the fact that the trade of Western Europe with this area is much more important than United States trade. We do about $200 million worth of trade with the entire Soviet bloc per annum. Western Europe does something like $5 billion, or twenty-five times as much. Obviously, restrictive policies on our part are not going to be very effective unless they are also the policies of Western European countries, and unless they are seriously and enthusiastically enforced. This is most unlikely to be the case. Certain important entities—namely, Sweden, Switzerland and Jugoslavia—are, of course, not embraced at all, even formally, in any system of NATO trade controls. But even those Western European countries that are so embraced often have somewhat different feelings about the whole procedure than we do. And commercial discipline throughout this area is not much more adequate today than it was in the 1920s and 1930s for the enforcement of trade restrictions which conflict strongly with the interests of tens of thousands of private traders. These disparities are already sharply reflected in the incongruity of the figures on United States trade with the bloc and that of Western Europe.

Despite this relatively high level of Western European exchanges with the bloc, a shadow falls today over the future of this trade, in the form of the potential internal protectionism of the countries of the European Common Market. These countries are willing enough, as a rule, to export to Eastern Europe; but to what extent they will continue to show themselves receptive to imports from that area, and particularly to imports of agricultural products, is another question. Anxieties on this score exist in several of the Eastern European countries, especially in Jugoslavia and Poland, both of which have an important stake in exports of agricultural commodities to Germany and other Common Market countries. These anxieties are perhaps somewhat exaggerated. But they are probably inevitable, particularly in the light of the fact that it seems to have been impossible for the governments of these countries, to date, to find anyone who would, or could, undertake to discuss responsibly, on behalf of the Common Market, the problems of their future trade with the countries of that area. They are left, in this way, to bat in the dark; and whoever bats in the dark normally has exaggerated fears.

Such anxieties are, of course, not peculiar to the countries of Eastern Europe. They are shared by a considerable number of governments across the globe, not to mention the European neutrals. But there is perhaps a special sensitivity in Eastern Europe by virtue of the political overtones that surround every question of this sort. This has been heightened by the fact that whereas a good deal of public discussion has been devoted in Western Europe to the question of relations between the Common Market and the European neutrals, the similar problem, as it affects the Eastern European countries, has received very little attention, particularly in Germany. In any case, the gravity of this problem for the Eastern European governments, as they face the difficult questions of orientation between East and West, is not appreciably mitigated by the fact that they have company in other parts of the world.

Here again, opinion as to what constitutes the American interest will be divided according to political outlooks. Those who wish to see the satellite countries, and Jugoslavia, deprived of possibilities other than those of a close and exclusive association with the Soviet Union and with each other, will no doubt welcome a Western European protectionism which tends to exclude Eastern European products from the Western markets; and they will continue to regard our own denial of normal tariff treatment to the Eastern European countries as a useful example to the countries of the Common Market. Those, on the other hand, who see value in the achievement by the satellites of a more flexible and independent position, which would permit them to develop trading relations with both East or West as their interests may suggest, will naturally look at it the other way.

So much for the background situation, in so far as the Soviet Union and the Communist countries of Eastern Europe are concerned. China and its satellite régimes in Asia constitute another problem again: one which resembles in many ways that presented by the Soviet régime in its infancy. But since the problems of trade with Russia and Eastern Europe today are probably closely akin to those of trade with China in the future, it may be permissible for purposes of this discussion to stick to the former.

𝕾𝕾𝕾

As ONE attempts, against the background of what has been outlined above, to think out the problems of policy which East–West trade presents for the United States at this juncture, certain broad considerations present themselves.

First, it must be recognized that the overriding values here involved are political rather than economic. Particularly is this true when it comes to United States trade with Russia and the bloc; for here the economic dimensions are entirely of a secondary order. But it is also true when it comes to the question of Western European policies in this field. For while the economic aspects of Western Europe's trade with the East are not negligible, and deserve respect in themselves, its most important aspect is really the effect it will have on the future orientations and policies of the Eastern European countries, and on their relations with one another and with the Soviet Union in particular. The problem of East–West trade is, in short, primarily a political problem, and should be approached as such.

Secondly, I think we should recognize that a policy designed primarily to throttle economic exchanges between the Soviet bloc and the West, as a means of impeding the military-industrial development of the Soviet Union, is simply not apt to be very successful, at least not in the sense of accomplishing anything more than to increase autarkic tendencies within the bloc as a whole and to slow down, to a minor and undecisive extent, the advance of the Soviet economy. It might be questioned whether even a total Western blockade of a region so vast and rich and possessing already so highly developed an industrial base as does the present Soviet bloc could really be effective in accomplishing more than this. In any case, to reduce East–West trade to a level which would have a major and decisive effect along these lines would require, at the least, something like a total Western blockade of the entire Communist orbit. But the effort to establish such a blockade would involve so severe a conflict with natural trading compulsions, and would place so heavy a burden on private as well as national economic interests, that the invitations to evasion would be ubiquitous, and the prospects for success would not be favorable even if the effort was one sponsored by the governments of *all* the major Western trading countries, and not just a portion of them.

In addition, it must be remembered that such an undertaking runs directly counter to the development of a healthy political and economic polycentrism within the bloc. Admittedly, there is as yet no adequate consensus, in the United States at least, as to whether such a polycentrism is what we wish to encourage. But it must be recognized that what is done in the field of trade policy is going to affect this situation one way or another, whether one wishes it to or not. And one should probably expect that the negative attitude toward this question—the view, that is, that polycentrism is *not* to be encouraged and that the West has most to gain by forcing the Communist countries in upon themselves economically—is one that is apt to encounter greater resistance in some European countries than it does in our own.

There is also a fundamental theoretical consideration on which a sharp division must be expected between important segments of American and European opinion. The distinction was mentioned above between normal trade, on the one hand, and such things as long-term credits on abnormally lenient terms or other forms of what is in reality "aid," on the other. Now the question exists as to whether normal trade with a Communist government should be regarded as a favor, extended by us to it, to be requited by concessions to us in the political field, or whether it should not. There are, of course, those who would say that where the law of supply and demand is permitted to operate normally, where value is only exchanged for value, no question of ulterior obligation is involved, and that there is no more reason why we should ask a Communist country to give us some sort of a political reward for permitting such trade to proceed than there is for them to expect the same thing of us. The British, I understand, now go even further, and hold that not even the extension of long-term credit should be regarded as a proper *quid pro quo* for political concessions. It is quite evident, on the other hand, that in the minds of a great many Americans, trade with a Communist country, even on normal commercial terms, represents an act of graciousness on our part for which we should demand political concessions in return. This view is based, as a rule, on the thesis that the scales of values which prevail on the world markets and which normally govern international commercial transactions do not accurately reflect the real extent to which political interests are served on both sides when trade takes place between a Communist country and a non-Communist one. This was the view, for example, of a special mission of the House of Representatives which visited Europe a year ago to study these problems.

We have here a difference as between influential segments of

American and European opinion, which, again, will not be easily overcome, particularly because the sacrifices implicit in the American view are ones which would fall much more heavily, economically, on the Europeans than they do on us. To demand political concessions as a *quid pro quo* for normal commercial transactions is, after all, only another way of renouncing trade altogether; for Communist countries will never yield to overt demands of this nature. And obviously, such a renunciation would come harder to some of the Europeans than it would to people in the United States.

But there is another sense in which the suggestion of a connection between trade and politics has greater substance. If Communist governments cannot be expected to give political concessions for specific trading deals, they have shown a disposition, particularly the Russians, to place a high value on the readiness of others to talk and negotiate, at the governmental level, on governmental measures designed to promote trade. It is evident that they regard such a disposition as having an important symbolic value; and more than once, in the history of Communist diplomacy, trade talks have evidently been regarded, and have served, as an important preliminary approach to more far-reaching political dealings. Western governments will do well to bear in mind, therefore, that even if one cannot expect specific commercial deals to be requited with political concessions, there may be times when a readiness on their part to discuss in a constructive manner with Soviet or other Communist representatives the possibilities for a development of commercial relations in general will be appreciated and reciprocated on the other side as important evidence of a desire to improve relations across the board.

With these considerations in mind, it is perhaps now permissible to ask one's self what the outlines of a sensible American policy might be.

〄〄〄

WHEN IT comes to the trade of the United States with the bloc, it seems to me that the first thing we could usefully do would be to relax and not to make such heavy sledding of it. In economic terms, this trade is still of minor importance. In the case of the Soviet Union, it amounted in 1961 to only one per cent of the total Soviet trade, and something like two-tenths of a per cent of ours. Communist countries are not going to be decisively benefitted if this trade increases somewhat; nor are they going to be importantly injured if we restrict it still further. The Soviet government is not going to fall if we deny it wheat; and the heavens are not going to fall if we permit wheat to be shipped. The amount of agony of decision addressed to this subject in recent months has been out of proportion to what was actually involved.

Secondly, it may as well be recognized that the emotional overtones which this subject carries for much of American opinion, added to the unresolved differences among us over basic questions of political policy toward the bloc, make it idle for us to think that we can approach the problem of our own role in East–West trade on the basis of a cool and detached appraisal of national interest. One does not need to argue about just what the configurations of a policy so calculated would be. Whatever they would be, if they involved any appreciable liberalization of what we have been doing in recent years, they would at once become controversial, particularly in Congressional opinion, to a degree that would militate greatly against their effectiveness. It is, in short, a matter in which we are simply incapable of acting at this time in any purely detached manner. For this, a calmer state of opinion would be necessary, and there would have to be a wider consensus on fundamental questions of policy. For the moment, therefore, anything in the way of a major relaxation of our export controls or extension of our commercial dealings with Russia and the bloc, has to be regarded as simply subjectively unfeasible. The Russians and the satellites will have to understand that if they have favorable chances at all for trade with the West, these chances do not lie in our direction—at least not until there is a marked and prolonged improvement in the political atmosphere.

On the other hand, it should, I think, be recognized that in view of the many variations in the way this problem presents itself to us—the differences, for example, between the considerations affecting trade with the Soviet Union and those affecting trade with the satellites, or between those prevailing in the case of Jugoslavia and those affecting trade with other Communist nations—it is not a problem which lends itself favorably to treatment by sweeping general determinations of policy, and particularly not in the form of legislative strictures. To deal in any way effectively with this problem, we need flexibility of approach— we need the ability to discriminate intelligently. Even a policy which is in essense one of denial or restriction of trade, should not be anchored in sweeping legislative injunctions which leave nobody—not even the legislative branch itself—in a position to make intelligent exceptions. It would be better to have a more restrictive and negative policy which rested on a firm understanding between Congressional leaders and the Executive but left somebody free to use his head when it needed to be used, than to try to pursue more liberal policies against the background of a jealous Congressional disposition to prescribe and limit their effects by legislative action.

When it comes to our attitude toward the trading policies of our associates in Western Europe, quite other considerations apply than do in the case of our own trade. Here, again, the best answer would seem to be: relax—but relax in the other direction. If at home the need is for a reduction of tension and controversy by accepting the internal compulsions that make it difficult for us to trade with the bloc, in the case of our European associates it is a question of accepting those external compulsions which make it difficult for them *not* to trade.

This is not to be taken as a suggestion that our European friends should be told that so far as we are concerned anything

goes, and that there are no measures of prudence we would con-
sider to be in order. There will still be need, of course, for agreement with them over the definition of what constitutes strategic
materials, unsuitable for release to a politically hostile government. There way well be, as in the case of Soviet oil shipments,
instances in which it will be necessary for us to take a sympathetic
attitude toward, or even associate ourselves with, measures of col-
lective defense, designed to prevent Western markets from being
dangerously affected by Soviet trading practices. But whether we
should try to bring pressure on the Western Europeans in matters
of normal trade with the Communist bloc is another matter. They
are not apt to agree entirely, no matter how hard we press, with
those outlooks in this country which place such heavy limitations
on our own ability to shape policy in this field. Their problems
are in many respects their own, not ours. And we, divided and
vacillating as we are in our basic judgments as to how to face the
problem of international Communism, are not apt to be very
helpful guides to others in the shaping of their economic policies
in the field of East–West trade.

Continued pressures on our European allies for the restriction
of their trade with the Soviet Union and the bloc are unlikely
to be very effective in hampering Soviet economic development.
But there are two other effects they *are* likely to have. The first,
which may be predicted with some confidence on the basis of
past experience, is to place further strain on our relations with
our European partners and to give us one more thing to disagree
and argue about. The second is to throw just enough uncertainty
into the minds of the Western Europeans to prevent them from
doing anything very effective on their own in the way of giving
Eastern Europe the alternative it needs, and to some extent is
seeking, to an exclusive economic association with the Soviet
bloc. To the extent that the Western Europeans are willing to
move in the direction of expanded East–West trade, it would not
seem to be our business to attempt to stop them, whatever our
own feelings. For the opposite concept, the one which sees Russia's economic advance being importantly impeded by something

like a Western blockade, is not going to work anyway beyond a point; and in moving to prevent the first one from being tried, even by our allies, we will simply be assuring that there can be no effective Western policy at all in this field: no effective policy of the denial of trade, because objective conditions do not permit it; no effective policy of its extension, because our pressures will be just sufficient to make it a half-hearted and half-way measure.

These are my reasons for suggesting that, while exercising in regard to our own trade with the East whatever restraint is necessary to retain a reasonably adequate consensus of opinion behind our policy, we reduce the claims we place on the policies of our various allies and associates throughout the world, and leave them greater freedom to decide for themselves what they want to do. This will ease our relationship with them. It will permit us to satisfy our own pangs of conscience about trading with a political antagonist. The loss to be suffered, in terms of the pace of Russia's economic advance, will not be great, even in the eyes of those who see our purposes advanced only by Russia's economic setbacks. And meanwhile, we will at least permit to be conducted, to the extent our Western European friends have the inclination to conduct it, an experiment in which many of us may not greatly believe but which it is unnecessary and perhaps dangerous for us to inhibit: whether, namely, the possibility of better trading opportunities with the West—for Russia, the possibility of a better international division of labor in the interests of her own economic advance; for the satellites, the prospects of a re-inclusion into the community of Europe in at least one important respect—whether this possibility will not have a useful effect on the Communist bloc as a whole, and produce such changes as to cause the entire problem of East–West trade to assume, eventually, a different and less forbidding aspect.

3
POLYCENTRISM
AND WESTERN POLICY

MUCH of the discussion in Western countries today of the problem of relations with world Communism centers around the recent disintegration of that extreme concentration of power in Moscow which characterized the Communist bloc in the immediate aftermath of the Second World War, and the emergence in its place of a plurality of independent or partially independent centers of political authority within the bloc: the growth, in other words, of what has come to be described as "polycentrism." There is widespread recognition that this process represents a fundamental change in the nature of world Communism as a political force on the world scene; and there is an instinctive awareness throughout Western opinion that no change of this order could fail to have important connotations for Western policy. But just what these connotations are is a question on which much uncertainty and confusion still prevail.

The historical development of the process of polycentrism, particularly as it has manifested itself in the growing differences between the Russian and Chinese Communists, is a subject to which a great deal of careful study has recently been devoted and on which there is already an excellent body of analytical literature. There is no need to attempt to recapitulate here the conclusions—remarkably unanimous, in the circumstances—at which leading scholars have arrived concerning the causes and course of this process. Suffice it to recall that it had its origins, generally speaking, in two great events of the year 1948: the forced defection of the Jugoslavs, and the Communist seizure of power in China.

The unity of the bloc never fully recovered from the shock of the Jugoslav defection. Had the Jugoslavs undergone something like a counterrevolution—had they shaken off their own Communist dictatorship, adopted a form of government which permitted democratic freedoms, and relaxed the governmental hold on the economy to a point where the system would have been no longer classifiable as a Leninist-Marxist one—the effect on bloc unity would have been less; for then the defection could have been regarded simply as the loss of a position to the capitalist world: a regrettable setback but not unprecedented, and no fit cause of doubt or questioning for a movement which had always prided itself on its ability to pocket losses and to recover from them. But when the Jugoslavs failed to do any of these things—when the Jugoslav Communist Party remained in power, and Jugoslavia did not go over to the capitalist camp but carried on much as before, claiming to be a Communist state and talking like one but not recognizing the discipline of the bloc or accepting any political obligations toward it—this was really unsettling for those who had remained faithful; for it raised the appalling question whether monolithic unity and discipline were essential at all to the development of Marxian socialism: whether one could not be a perfectly good Communist without taking orders blindly from Moscow and without following slavishly the pattern of institutions and methods established by the Soviet Union.

And since the strains of Stalinist rule were greater in the more Westernized states of the satellite area of Eastern Europe than in Russia itself, this suggestion—that there might be more than one path to socialism—was particularly insidious in its effect on the satellite régimes. Many were the satellite Communists who, in the years following Tito's break with Stalin, groaned under the necessity of pursuing Stalinist policies obviously unfitted to the traditions and psychology of their country and stole envious looks at the Jugoslavs, who could now cut their cloth to suit their own figure and yet maintain the claim to be good Marxian socialists. It is instructive to reflect that precisely that feature of Jugoslav behavior which so many Americans today find it impossible to forgive, namely, that the Jugoslavs did not, so to speak, "go capitalist," but carried on as a Marxian-socialist state, was the factor which more than any other proved disrupting in its effect on bloc unity.

So long as Stalin remained alive, the effects of the Jugoslav defection could be reasonably well contained by the Moscow headquarters. But after his death, this proved no longer possible. The de-Stalinization campaign of the mid-fifties implied at least a partial justification of Tito's earlier defiance of Stalin's authority. It was awkward, in these circumstances, to leave the Jugoslavs wholly outside the camp; and Khrushchev felt it necessary to try to draw them back again—something which could be done only by conciliatory means. But this, implying as it did at least a willingness to forgive the earlier Jugoslav defiance of bloc discipline, proved unsettling in its effect on the other satellites, particularly the Poles and Hungarians, and had a good deal to do with the events of 1956 in those two countries. For the Polish and Hungarian Communists had to ask themselves: if Tito is to be forgiven and treated with deference, where are the rewards of obedience? Why should not we, too, select our own path?

As for China, rivalry between the Soviet and Chinese Communist régimes was latent from the beginning, but it began to appear on the surface only after Stalin's death; and it was not until 1957 that it began to assume forms which threatened seriously to disturb bloc unity. It is interesting to reflect that it was in part differing reactions to these same events of 1956 that caused the Chinese-Soviet disagreements to become acute. For what the Russians found necessary in absorbing the shock and the lessons of Hungary proved intolerable to the Chinese, whose revolution was in a different stage and who had different political needs. Here is seen how one thing leads to another, how the threads of causality lead on from the original Jugoslav disaffection and the Chinese Communist conquest of China in 1948—the one considered at the time a loss to world Communism, the other a victory—to the polycentrism of today. If there is any lesson in this, it is the demonstration of how poor we all are, even the Communists, at knowing what is a victory and what is a defeat.

We are now confronted with a situation in which what was once a unified and disciplined bloc has disintegrated into something more like an uneasy alliance between two ideologically similar commonwealths: one grouped around the Soviet Union, the other around China. But even that element of order and symmetry which this description would suggest is not complete, because one nominally Communist country, Jugoslavia, is not embraced in either of these alliances, and another, Albania, is nominally and formally embraced in the one (it still belongs to the Warsaw Pact) but is politically closer to the other. And beyond this framework, there are a large number of Communist parties not in power which are greatly torn and bewildered by this division; and some of these parties have an important voice in bloc affairs, even though they lack the prestige that comes of being in power in their respective countries.

Barring unforeseen disturbances in international affairs, I think this state of affairs should be expected to endure, in its essential aspects, for a long time. Efforts will be made, of course, at one point or another, to patch up Soviet-Chinese differences and to restore something like the previous unity. The Poles, who have always had a special hankering for close relations with the Chinese Communists, are apt to be particularly assiduous in trying to assuage the Chinese-Soviet differences. Perhaps at some point changes of personalities in Moscow and Peking will help. But such tendencies can scarcely go beyond a point. An attempt to establish either Moscow or Peking as the unchallenged center of the movement would today involve prohibitive strains. Communism has now come to embrace so wide a spectrum of requirements and compulsions on the part of the respective parties and régimes that any determined attempt to re-impose unity on the movement would merely cause it to break violently apart at one point or another. There can scarcely be any meeting ground today between, say, the Chinese Communist Party and the Communist Party of Italy that would not be disastrous to one or the other.

A complete restoration of unity seems therefore to be out. But a total break, to the point of all-out hostilities and the alliance of one or the other faction with parts of the non-Communist world, seems equally improbable. Excruciating as are the differences which have now developed within the world Communist camp, all of the disputants are aware that they have nothing to gain, and everything to lose, by tearing themselves to pieces for the benefit of the "imperialists." Chinese and Russians, furthermore, are both highly skilled at the delicate gradating of hostilities of every sort; and while it would not be surprising to see at some point the development of armed conflicts along the Soviet-Chinese frontier comparable in seriousness to those that developed between the Russians and the Japanese along the same frontier in 1938, it would be surprising to see them develop, any more than did those of 1938, into a full-fledged state of war between the disputants.

ᔕᔕᔕ

WHILE this state of affairs, is then, likely to last for some time in its major outlines, it allows of considerable variation and evolution in terms of the relations between various Communist countries and the non-Communist world. This is a point of great flux and uncertainty throughout the bloc. Not only do the Chinese-Soviet differences center around disagreements over this point, and not only are there further differences on this score between the Russians and individual satellite states of Eastern Europe, but almost every Communist party in the world is afflicted by sharp internal differences or gradations of opinion along these lines. It is not too much to say that the entire bloc is caught today in a great crisis of indecision over the basic question of the proper attitude of a Communist country toward non-Communist ones. The question is whether to think of the world in terms of an irreconcilable and deadly struggle between all that calls itself Communist and all that does not, a struggle bound to end in the relatively near future with the total destruction of one or both, or to recognize that the world socialist cause can be advanced by more complicated, more gradual, less dramatic and less immediate forms, not necessitating any effort to destroy all that is not Communist within our time, and even permitting, in the meanwhile, reasonably extensive and profitable and durable relations with individual non-Communist countries.

The lines of division of opinion over this issue are by no means clean; very often both viewpoints struggle against each other in the same troubled Communist breast. But this is in essence the question. It is this which is buried under the long ideological arguments as to whether socialism could conceivably, or could not conceivably, be achieved by means that did not involve violent revolution. It is this that underlies the arguments about the inevitability or non-inevitability of war. This is the explosive substance with which the controversial concept of "peaceful coexistence" is charged. And none of us, I am sure, can fail to note that this is only the mirror-replica of the similar question which divides Western public opinion and tortures the policy-makers of the Western countries.

It is important to recognize that the degree to which polycentrism has already advanced means that individual Communist countries now have a far wider area of choice than was the case some years ago in shaping not only their own relationship to the non-Communist world but also their internal institutions and policies. These two things are, in fact, closely connected; for the more internal institutions and policies come to resemble those that once prevailed in Stalin's Russia and/or prevail today in China, the more one needs a state of apparent tension and danger in external relations, as a means of justifying them. And in both these fields, as I say, the smaller Communist countries, and particularly the Eastern European satellites, now enjoy a far wider range of independent decision than was once the case. At one time there was only one model; today there are a number of them: the Soviet, the Chinese, the Polish, the Jugoslav, etc. And the fact that Moscow and Peking both need the political support of the satellite parties, and are therefore obligated to compete for their favor, means that neither can afford to discipline them, beyond a point, if the paths they choose are not ones that meet with full approval on either side.

On the other hand, the area within which this freedom of choice exists is not unlimited; it has, in fact, certain very sharp limits, and it is important to bear these in mind.

The satellite régimes of Eastern Europe cannot, first of all, sever the bonds of military alliance which unite them with the Russians. Jugoslavia, it is true, did this in effect; but one must remember that when this occurred, the Warsaw Pact did not yet exist—nor did the Atlantic Alliance. Further, the Jugoslavs had a very special geographic and political position.

Secondly, the satellite régimes cannot abandon the profession of fidelity to Marxist ideals or the monopoly of power which those ideals imply and purport to justify. To do anything like this would be to destroy the very theoretical basis on which their power rests, and to commit, in effect, political suicide.

What the satellite régimes *can* do, and are doing to some extent, is to shape their own internal economic and social institutions along more liberal lines, or at least individualistic lines. They can, furthermore, ease the restraints—as the Jugoslavs have done— on all forms of contact and dealings between their citizens and people in non-Communist countries. As a part of this process, they can resist—as the Rumanians are doing—efforts to pull them into a tight and exclusive trading association with other Communist countries; and they can insist on the right to expand their trade with non-Communist nations to a point where it constitutes an important element in their economic development.

Finally, while they cannot leave the Communist military alliance, the satellite régimes could, conceivably, if conditions were right, help to deëmphasize the military factor to a point where it would not stand in the way of at least a partial political rapprochement with some of their Western neighbors.

Altogether, then, the choices open to the satellite régimes cover a range which lies somewhere between the extremes of the full independence of the Jugoslavs on the one hand, and a slavish, timid clinging to Soviet patterns and authority on the other. This is a circumscribed range of choice; but what they do within it is by no means unimportant. It could, conceivably, make all the difference between a Communist orbit with which the West could coexist peacefully and without catastrophe over an indefinite time, and one with which it could not.

<p align="center">~~~</p>

Now the West has it in its power, ideally speaking, to influence extensively, by its own policies and behavior, the choices that the satellite régimes make in this connection. It can reciprocate or fail to reciprocate moves to relax tensions and to facilitate collaboration in various fields. It can shape its policies in such a way as to create advantages and premiums for efforts on the part of the satellite governments to extend their relations with Western countries; or it can decline to create such advantages. It can exert itself to deëmphasize the military factor in the mutual relationship; or it can take the opposite course. Finally, and of overriding significance, it can show itself reconciled to the existence of these régimes, without accepting responsibility for them; and it can convey to them that they have nothing to fear from it if they will only refrain, themselves, from hostile and subversive policies; or it can hold to the thesis that its object is to overthrow them, and permit them to conclude that any concessions they may make will only be exploited, ultimately, to their disadvantage.

Obviously, in the totality of these choices, the West is confronted by a pervasive and fundamental problem of policy: whether to promote a trend toward further polycentrism, in the hope that there might prove to be a portion of the Communist world with which one could, in the long run, contrive to live, and that living with it and encouraging it to see advantages in a situation of coexistence might tend at least to narrow the area and power of that other portion with which one could not live, or could not *yet* live; or whether to discourage that trend, on the theory that a differentiation of outlook and authority among Communist powers does not materially affect their status as a threat to the security of the Western peoples, and that the impression of such a differentiation serves merely to disorient and demoralize Western resistance to the phenomenon of world Communism as a whole. This is the question facing Western policy-makers; and there can in my opinion be no doubt that the trend of political decision within the Communist world will be importantly influenced by the answers they find to it. It could well be argued, in fact, that if the major Western powers had full freedom of movement in devising their own policies, it would be within their power to determine whether the Chinese view, or the Soviet view, or perhaps a view more liberal than either, would ultimately prevail within the Communist camp.

Fortunately, or unfortunately, the major Western powers do not enjoy this full freedom of movement. In the case particularly of the United States and Western Germany, but also to some extent of the NATO powers in general, the area in which they could conceivably move to meet the problem of policy posed by the trend toward Communist polycentrism has been severely circumscribed in recent years either by engagements they have undertaken to one another or to parties outside of Europe or by policies to which they have so deeply committed themselves that any early renunciation of them would scarcely be feasible. A glance at their position with relation to the various points of flexibility in the position of the satellite régimes will suffice to demonstrate this.

If it is a question of alteration of the internal institutions and policies of the satellite régimes, it is evident, on the example of Jugoslavia, that neither the United States Congress nor the West German Government is inclined to attach importance to this factor. The Jugoslavs have abolished forced collectivization. They have adopted a system of management in industry fundamentally different from that prevailing in the Soviet Union. They have practically abandoned the active application of police terror. They have adopted policies on travel, contacts with foreigners and access to foreign informational media which seem closer to those of most Western countries than to those prevalent in the bloc. It is evident that none of this constitutes, in the eyes of our own Congress or of a great part of our public, any reason to treat Jugoslavia very much differently from any other Communist country. A similar disposition seems to prevail in Bonn, if only as a reflection of the Hallstein doctrine, which bars diplomatic relations with any country recognizing the present East German régime. Since all of the satellites do recognize it, they are obliged to see in this doctrine at least a limitation to the possibilities of any future political rapprochement between themselves and the German Federal Republic.

When it comes to economic policy, a similar situation prevails. There are the NATO arrangements for economic controls. There are the various legislative restrictions prevailing in this country. There is, finally, the Common Market, established and being developed on principles that appear to leave no room for anything like the eventual economic reunification of the European Continent. It will be recalled that in the original Marshall Plan concept, American policy-makers were careful to leave open the possibility of the extension of the respective arrangements to the entire Continent, and to phrase the proposals in such a way that if the Eastern European régimes were to be excluded, they would have to exclude themselves, which, in effect, they then did. But the European Common Market has failed to include this feature either in letter or in spirit; and the impression is being given to the Eastern Europeans, including the Jugoslavs, that whatever may be the future of this novel and important entity, they are to have no place in it.

When it comes to the military factor and the question of its emphasis or deëmphasis, the bald fact is that the Western powers,

over a period that now runs back for several years, have committed themselves more and more deeply against anything in
the nature of a military disengagement in Europe. Not only do
they reject the possibility of any extensive withdrawal of foreign
troops from the Western part of the Continent, even if this were
to be by way of reciprocation for a similar withdrawal of Soviet
forces, but they appear to have set their face, in present circumstances, against anything in the nature of a European pact or a
nonaggression pact between the NATO and Warsaw Pact members. They are also averse to any sort of arrangement for the
de-nuclearization of the European area, even, again, if this were
to be on a reciprocal basis. Finally, they have exhibited no very
convincing evidence of any disposition to place effective limits
on the rearmament of Western Germany, where one restriction
after the other, established in earlier years, has quietly gone
by the board, and where the Germans are now, in the view
of everybody in Eastern Europe, well on the way to becoming
in all essential respects a full-fledged nuclear power. Yet at the
same time the Western powers, with the exception of the French,
have been unwilling to recognize the finality of Germany's eastern frontiers; and the West German Government, with the blessing of the others, still pursues a policy of total irreconcilability
toward the East German state.

These aspects of Western policy are not mentioned for the
purpose of taking issue with them. Opinions can differ on the
degree of their justification, individually or collectively. But even
those who are enthusiastic about them should remember that
there is a price to be paid for them in terms of their political effect
on the Communist bloc. To the East European satellite leaders,
faced with these attitudes, and noting the extreme rigidity with
which they are adhered to by the Western governments, anything
like a deëmphasis of the military factor in East–West relations
can only appear today as discouragingly remote. In present circumstances, they can hope neither for the removal of Soviet forces
from those Eastern European positions which they now occupy,
nor for any further East–West agreements that could take the

heat off military tensions. Particularly discouraging and disturb-ing to them is the progressive rearmament of Western Germany against the background of a West German commitment to the liberation of Eastern Germany, even though that commitment professes to envisage only peaceful means. The effect which the combination of these two things has had on the feelings of people in Eastern Europe cannot be emphasized too strongly. Either one without the other might have been less unacceptable. A strong commitment to the reunification of Germany might have been tolerable if it had not been supported by a military policy de-signed to make Western Germany into one of the two strongest states in Western Europe. Or a rearmament of Western Germany, while never fully defensible in East European eyes, might have been more tolerable if it had been coupled with a greater readi-ness on the part of West German political leaders to *faire bonne mine à mauvais jeu*, to accept the existence of a Communist Germany at least as a regrettable necessity of the present epoch, and to regard the cause of German unification less as a program-matical commitment and more as an historical inevitability, to be left to the healing hand of time. But the spectre of the violent liberation of Eastern Germany, by means not resting on any agreement with the Russians, and coming either against the back-ground of, or by means of, a revived German military ascendancy, unites both governments and peoples in Eastern Europe in a common reaction of horror and apprehension; for the Communist leaders there, however little they may like or respect Ulbricht, know that their own stability would not easily withstand the shock of the sudden and violent overthrow of his régime; and the peoples of Eastern Europe, including the Jugoslavs, see in this eventuality only the beginning of a reëstablishment of the Ger-man military ascendancy of unhappy memory throughout East-ern Europe, and 18 years have not been sufficient to allow the horror of this prospect to fade in their minds.

Behind all this, and connected with all of it, is the heavy ex-tent of the Western commitment, and particularly the American and German commitment, to the eventual destruction of Communism generally. We have our Captive Nations Resolution; and the satellite régimes of Eastern Europe and Asia are specifically listed there as ones we have committed ourselves in effect to destroy. In the Far East, there is our similar commitment to the Nationalist Government on Taiwan, with all its far-reaching political ambitions. And Western opinion, not just in the NATO countries but in certain of the neutral European countries as well, is heavily affected by attitudes which are at least skeptical toward, and in some cases strongly averse to, any thought of an accommodation to the permanency of Communist power anywhere.

It is true that the West European NATO governments are in a somewhat better position to face this problem than is the United States. They are not committed to the Captive Nations Resolution. There is no formal reason why they should not, if they wished, shape the policies of the Common Market in such a way as to give to the Eastern European peoples a more reassuring impression of the prospects for their future relation to Western Europe in the economic field. In the case of export controls and other restrictive measures, the degree of their responsibility is obviously smaller than ours; and it would, presumably, be easier for them to take a more conciliatory line. Particularly is all this true of the Italians, whose understanding attitude has already helped to ease Jugoslavia's delicate relations with the West, and who, more than any other Western people, have possibilities for exerting a reassuring and helpful influence on the East European satellites. But further north, the German problem and the aversion to any discussion of disengagement still loom up on the horizon of the Eastern Europeans as impassable barriers to anything like such a lowering of tensions as would make it possible for them to create a basically new political relationship with the West; and for both of these situations, as they well know, Western Europeans are as responsible as ourselves.

It is clear, in these circumstances, that the West has, as of today, only limited possibilities for reciprocating any disposition the satellite countries might evince to reduce the dichotomy of the two worlds and to bridge the gap that divides present attitudes on both sides from the possibility of truly peaceful and mutually profitable coexistence. It is in a sense tragic that this should be the case just at a time when there is so great a longing for a better East–West relationship in the hearts of tens of millions of ordinary people in the East European area, and so important a willingness to move tentatively in this direction even on the part of certain of their Communist leaders. And the fact that things are this way is something which should give pause for thought not just to those who would like to find ways of living peacefully with Communist neighbors but even to those who can contemplate no permanent reconciliation with world Communism; for to deny to the East even the possibility of the development of a better framework for coexistence is to affect the terms of the argument which goes on within the Communist camp and to forego the advantage which a division of opinion there provides. If there is really strength in unity, Communist leaders can only be grateful for a Western policy which slights the values of polycentrism and declines to encourage them; for a rigidly unreceptive Western attitude may eventually enforce upon the bloc a measure of unity which, by their own unaided effort, they could never have achieved.

To say that the West is in a poor position to encourage polycentrism is not, of course, to say that it will not continue to develop. There are instances in which, as in the case of Jugoslavia, the desire for national independence may be so strong that governments will wish for, and seek, relief from the disciplinary strictures of the bloc even if there is no apparent place for them, or even for good relations with them, in the Western scheme of things; and it is not to be assumed that they will find no means of achieving that relief. The West, after all, does not represent the entirety of the non-Communist world. There are other areas where the trauma of the conflict with world Communism have struck less deeply and where both the readiness to forget or ignore ideological differences and the willingness to look at international relations in terms other than those of military conflict will be greater; and people who feel the need of more independence of policy but see no place for themselves in the vision of Western statesmanship can look, as the Jugoslavs are already doing, in other directions for the alternative to isolation.

Polycentrism may thus continue to develop, in spite of, if not because of, the face which the West turns to the troubled and vacillating world of Communism. But there are risks involved here. There is a relatively short-term risk, from the standpoint of the danger of war and of the effect which an absence of polycentrism could have in increasing that danger. But even if military complications do not ensue, there is still the long-term question of the effect on the minds of those tens of millions of people in Communist countries who still look to the West with longing and with hope and who expect from it policies which take account of all the subtlety and contradiction of their position. If such a response on the Western side is not forthcoming, who can say how this will affect their attitudes in the more distant future? Will they be best influenced by a Western policy which, through its quixotic commitment to a highly unlikely violent liberation, appears to condemn them by implication either to the miseries of a new world war or to an indefinite further period of languishing under oppressive Communist régimes? Or will they be better influenced by a Western policy which accepts as its goal the less ambitious but more promising prospect of a relaxation of the severity of those régimes and, by the same token, of the barriers that separate their peoples from contact with the outside world? This is a question which Western policy-makers will do well to look at all over again, as the Chinese-Soviet conflict proceeds and as its effects continue to make themselves felt.

In the nineteenth century, the colonial mother-countries of the West alienated many millions of people in other parts of the world through lack of imagination and feeling toward those who were in effect within their power. There is, surely, a danger lest history record that Westerners of the twentieth century alienated just as many more through lack of imagination and feeling toward those who were in the power of their ideological adversaries.

INDEX

Albania, 40
Atlantic Alliance, 43; *see also* NATO export controls

Battle Act, 24
Bolshevism, 10
Bullitt, William C., 3

Captive Nations Resolutions, 12–13, 19, 49
China, Nationalist (Taiwan), and U.S. liberation policy, 49
China, People's Republic of, 20, 38
and trade, 29
and U.S.S.R.; *see* Sino-Soviet dispute
Coexistence
desirability of, 5, 7, 10–15, 17–20, 44–45, 50–51
and East European satellites, 42, 44
and East-West trade, 26, 28–32
and German unification, 49
U.S. policy on, 5, 19–20, 49
vs. "victory," 6, 18
and Western policy, 45, 49–50
Common Market, European; *see* European Economic Community
Communism
defense against, 7
destruction of, 48–49
and political alternatives, 11
and U.S. policy toward, 7

Communist doctrine
paths to socialism, 42
peaceful coexistence, 41, 42
war, 42
Cuban crisis, 14

De-nuclearization of Europe, 47
Disengagement, policy of, 43–44, 47, 49

East European satellites
and coexistence, 42, 44
and German rearmament, 47–49
and German unification, 48, 49
Jugoslavia and, 38–39
liberalization in, 42–43, 50
Moscow and, 42–43
Peking and, 42–43
popular revolt, 11
Western trade restrictions, 46
East-West trade
complexity of problem, 24
and East European satellites, 21, 26–27
history of, 21–23
improvement of East-West relations, 32
political significance of, 28–32
private business and, 22–23, 27
strategic materials, 35
U.S. policy, 22, 24, 29, 30
volume of, before World War II, 23
Western policy on, 22, 24, 27, 29, 31

Publications of the Council on Foreign Relations

FOREIGN AFFAIRS (quarterly), edited by Hamilton Fish Armstrong.

THE UNITED STATES IN WORLD AFFAIRS (annual). Volumes for 1931, 1932 and 1933, by Walter Lippmann and William O. Scroggs; for 1934–1935, 1936, 1937, 1938, 1939 and 1940, by Whitney H. Shepardson and William O. Scroggs; for 1945–1947, 1947–1948 and 1948–1949, by John C. Campbell; for 1949, 1950, 1951, 1952, 1953 and 1954, by Richard P. Stebbins; for 1955, by Hollis W. Barber; for 1956, 1957, 1958, 1959, 1960, 1961 and 1962, by Richard P. Stebbins.

DOCUMENTS ON AMERICAN FOREIGN RELATIONS (annual). Volume for 1952 edited by Clarence W. Baier and Richard P. Stebbins; for 1953 and 1954, edited by Peter V. Curl; for 1955, 1956, 1957, 1958 and 1959, edited by Paul E. Zinner; for 1960, 1961 and 1962, edited by Richard P. Stebbins.

POLITICAL HANDBOOK AND ATLAS OF THE WORLD (annual), edited by Walter H. Mallory.

AFRICA: A Foreign Affairs Reader, edited by Philip W. Quigg.

THE PHILIPPINES AND THE UNITED STATES: Problems of Partnership, by George E. Taylor.

SOUTHEAST ASIA IN UNITED STATES POLICY, by Russell H. Fifield.

UNESCO: ASSESSMENT AND PROMISE, by George N. Shuster.

THE PEACEFUL ATOM IN FOREIGN POLICY, by Arnold Kramish.

THE ARABS AND THE WORLD: Nasser's Arab Nationalist Policy, by Charles D. Cremeans.

TOWARD AN ATLANTIC COMMUNITY, by Christian A. Herter.

THE SOVIET UNION, 1922–1962: A Foreign Affairs Reader, edited by Philip E. Mosely.

THE POLITICS OF FOREIGN AID: American Experience in Southeast Asia, by John D. Montgomery.

SPEARHEADS OF DEMOCRACY: Labor in the Developing Countries, by George C. Lodge.

LATIN AMERICA: Diplomacy and Reality, by Adolf A. Berle.

THE ORGANIZATION OF AMERICAN STATES AND THE HEMISPHERE CRISIS, by John C. Dreier.

THE UNITED NATIONS: Structure for Peace, by Ernest A. Gross.

THE LONG POLAR WATCH: Canada and the Defense of North America, by Melvin Conant.

Publications of the Council on Foreign Relations

ARMS AND POLITICS IN LATIN AMERICA (Revised Edition), by Edwin Lieuwen.

THE FUTURE OF UNDERDEVELOPED COUNTRIES: Political Implications of Economic Development (Revised Edition), by Eugene Staley.

SPAIN AND DEFENSE OF THE WEST: Ally and Liability, by Arthur P. Whitaker.

SOCIAL CHANGE IN LATIN AMERICA TODAY: Its Implications for United States Policy, by Richard N. Adams, John P. Gillin, Allan R. Holmberg, Oscar Lewis, Richard W. Patch, and Charles W. Wagley.

FOREIGN POLICY: THE NEXT PHASE: The 1960s (Revised Edition), by Thomas K. Finletter.

DEFENSE OF THE MIDDLE EAST: Problems of American Policy (Revised Edition), by John C. Campbell.

COMMUNIST CHINA AND ASIA: Challenge to American Policy, by A. Doak Barnett.

FRANCE, TROUBLED ALLY: De Gaulle's Heritage and Prospects, by Edgar S. Furniss, Jr.

THE SCHUMAN PLAN: A Study in Economic Cooperation, 1950–1959, by William Diebold, Jr.

SOVIET ECONOMIC AID: The New Aid and Trade Policy in Under-developed Countries, by Joseph S. Berliner.

RAW MATERIALS: A Study of American Policy, by Percy W. Bidwell.

NATO AND THE FUTURE OF EUROPE, by Ben T. Moore.

AFRICAN ECONOMIC DEVELOPMENT, by William Hance.

INDIA AND AMERICA: A Study of Their Relations, by Phillips Talbot and S. L. Poplai.

JAPAN BETWEEN EAST AND WEST, by Hugh Borton, Jerome B. Cohen, William J. Jorden, Donald Keene, Paul F. Langer and C. Martin Wilbur.

NUCLEAR WEAPONS AND FOREIGN POLICY, by Henry A. Kissinger.

MOSCOW-PEKING AXIS: Strengths and Strains, by Howard L. Boorman, Alexander Eckstein, Philip E. Mosely and Benjamin Schwartz.

RUSSIA AND AMERICA: Dangers and Prospects, by Henry L. Roberts.

FOREIGN AFFAIRS BIBLIOGRAPHY, 1942–1952, by Henry L. Roberts.